My name is ______________________.

Draw a picture of your favourite funny character from a story.

____
(character name)

____
(story title)

Handwriting: anticlockwise ellipse, short letter (u).
Grammar: nouns, action verbs, adverbs, antonyms (did/undid), question, question word (What?), word families (undo/undid/undone/undoing).
Punctuation: question mark, upper-case letter to start a sentence.

Spelling and vocabulary: prefix un- (undid, undo, untidily, untying, unzip), suffixes -ing, -ily (untying, untidily), umbrella, under, unicorn, upend.
Literary elements: riddle, joke, homophone word play (rain/rein).

Trace and finish the pattern.

Write the date.

Find and trace u and U.

u u W U n m V u U e U a o u u N

Trace then write.

What animal needs to

stand under an umbrella?

A reindeer.

Self assessment

How many u's have you written on this page?

Circle your best u.

Handwriting: anticlockwise ellipse, long letter (y).
Grammar: nouns, saying verbs (yell, yelled, cry, yodelling), adverb (yappily), tense (yell/yelled), question, question word (Where?).
Punctuation: question mark, upper-case letter to start a sentence.

Spelling and vocabulary: barking, parking, try, cry, yak, yappily, yawn, yelled, yodelling, suffixes -ing, -ily, -ed (barking, yappily, yelled). The word "yowie" is from the Yuwaalaraay language.
Literary elements: rhyme (cry/try, barking/parking), riddle, joke, word play (barking/parking).

Trace and finish the pattern.

Write the date.

Trace then write.

Where can you leave

your dog while you shop?

In the barking lot.

Circle the y with the best tail on these two pages.
Underline the y's you could have done better.

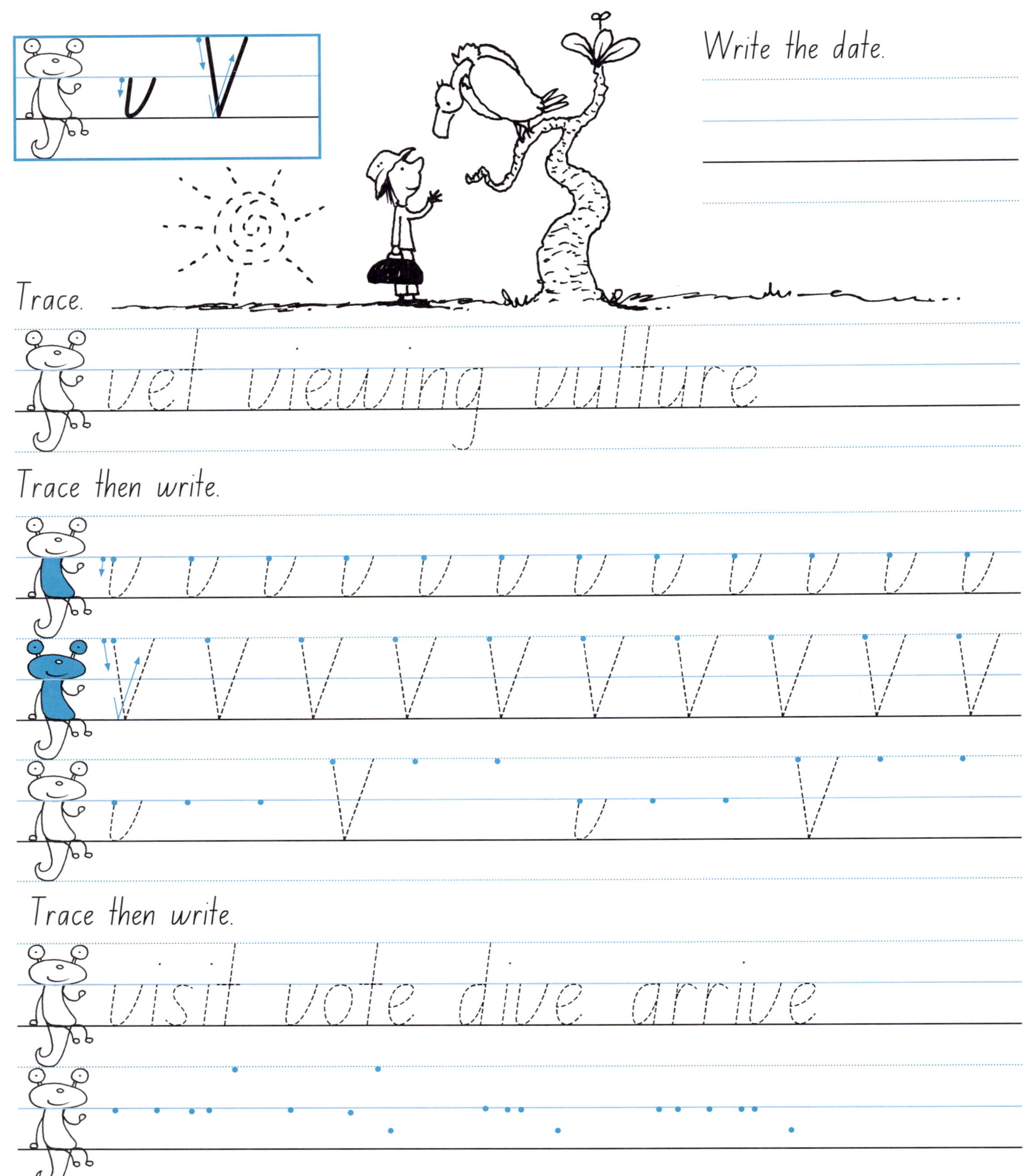

Handwriting: anticlockwise ellipse, short letter (v).
Grammar: nouns, action verbs (viewing, visit, vote, dive, arrive), statement.
Punctuation: full stop, upper-case letter to start a sentence.

Spelling and vocabulary: arrive, dive, brave, grave, save, behave, vet, viewing, visit, vote, vulture.
Literary elements: rhyme (arrive/dive/drive/survive, behave/brave/gave/save), Aesop (Greek) fable 'The Four Oxen and the Lion', moral: United we stand, divided we fall.

Trace and finish the pattern.

Write the date.

Write.

v

Use v to finish these words. Trace the words.

sa e bra e ga e beha e

Trace then write.

United we stand,

divided we fall.

Are each of your v's the same size?

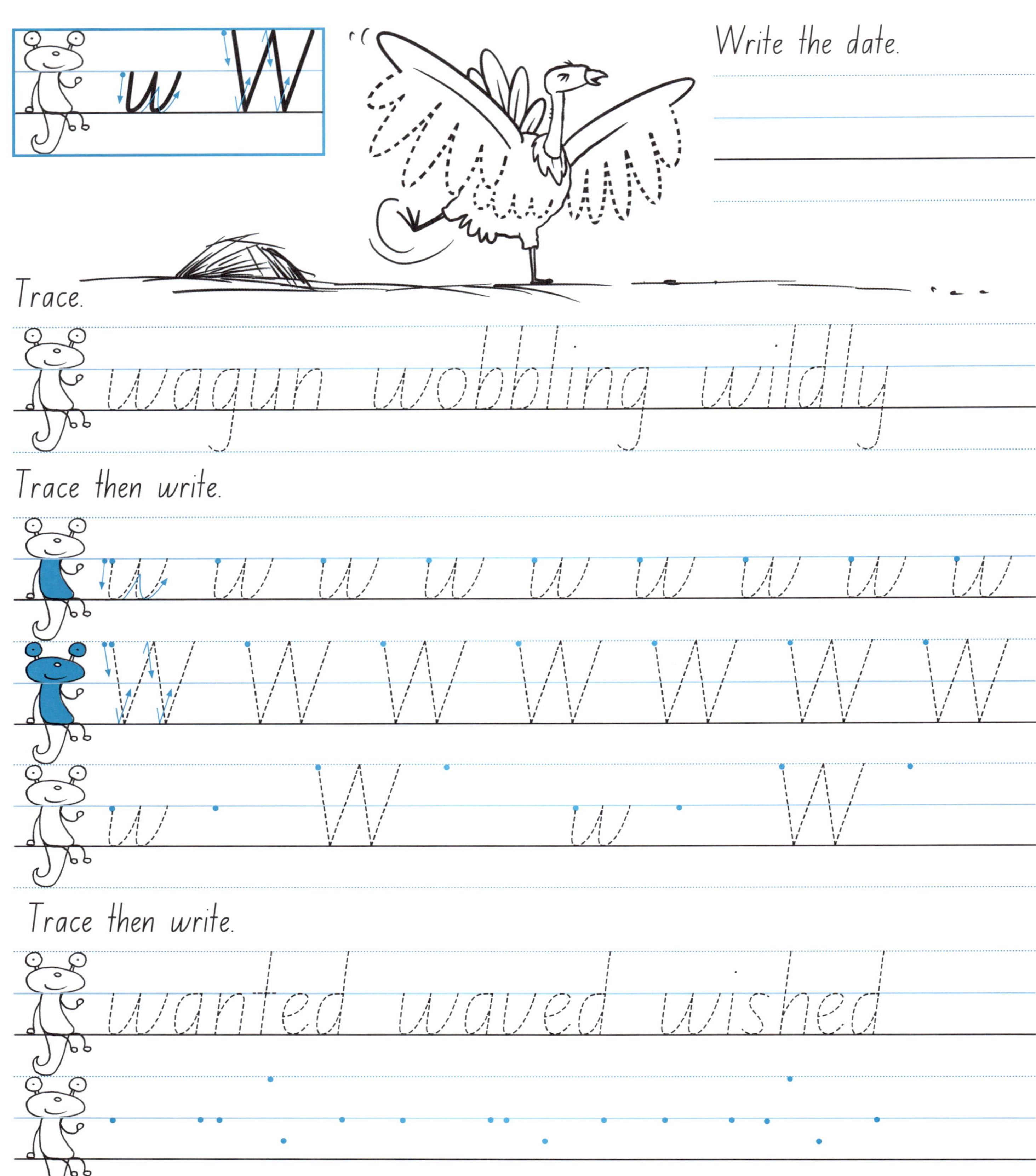

Handwriting: anticlockwise ellipse, short letter (w).
Grammar: proper noun (Wendy), sensing or thinking verbs (wanted, wished), adverb (wildly), past tense (waved, wished), question, question word (Why?).
Punctuation: question mark, upper-case letter to start a sentence.

Spelling and vocabulary: 'ow' (throw, window), wagun, 'a' for short 'o' sound (wanted, watch), suffixes -ing, -ly, -ed (wobbling, wildly, wished, waved). The word "wagun" is from the Bundjalung language. It means "brush turkey".
Literary elements: riddle, joke, homonym word play (wrist watch/watch time fly).

Trace and finish the pattern.

Write the date.

Trace then write.

Why did Wendy throw her

watch out the window?

To see time fly.

Draw a square around the word that is your best handwriting on these two pages.

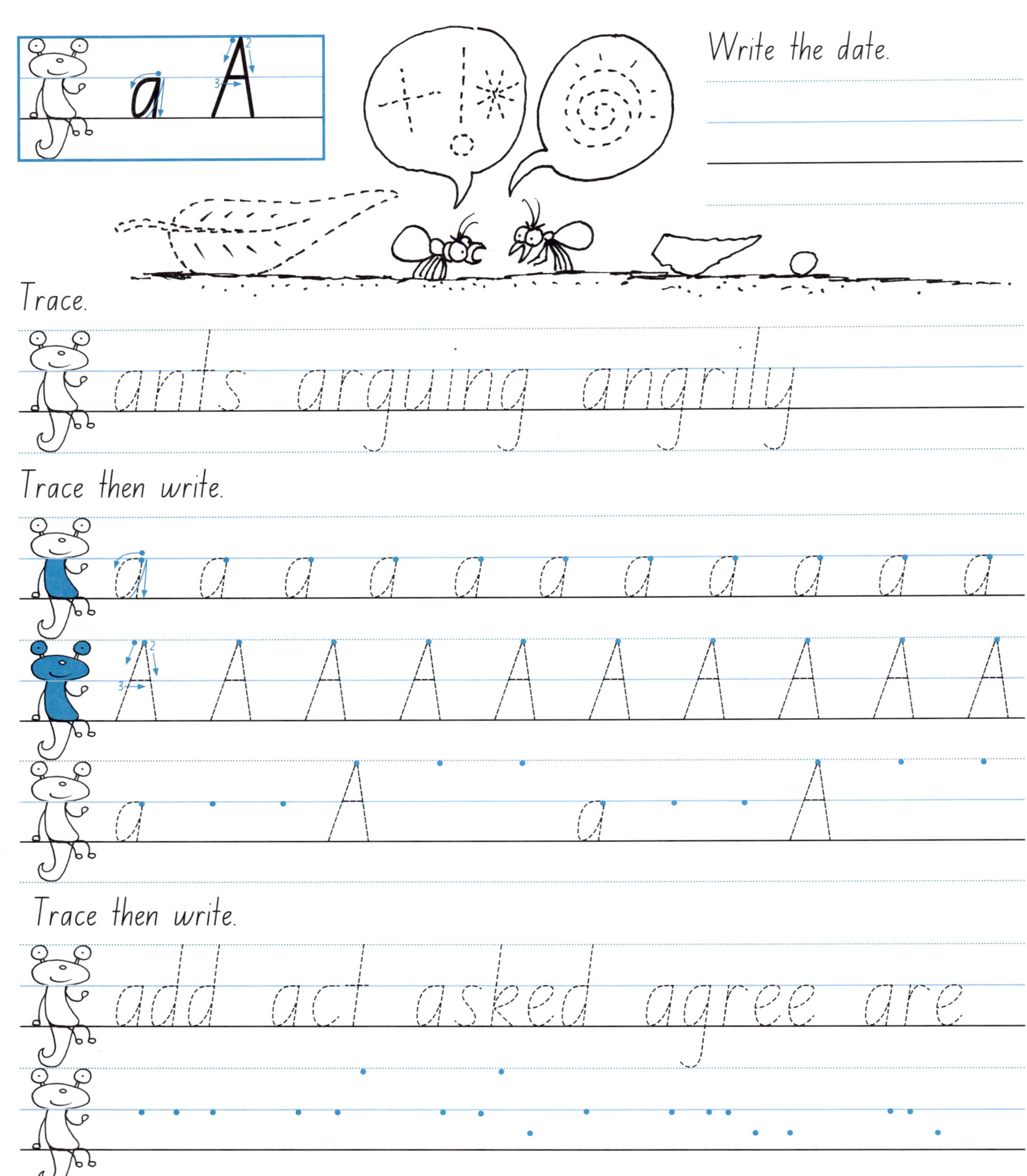

Handwriting: anticlockwise ellipse, short letter (a).
Grammar: nouns, saying verbs (agree, arguing, ask), adverb (angrily), statement.
Punctuation: full stop, upper-case letter to start a sentence.

Spelling and vocabulary: act, add, agree, angrily, ant, ape, apple, are, arguing, asked, away, day, today.
Literary elements: rhyme (away/day), proverb (Eat an apple on going to bed and you'll keep the doctor from earning his bread – Welsh proverb).

Trace and finish the pattern.

Write the date.

Write.

a A

Use a to finish these words. Trace the words.

pe w y go tod y d y

Trace then write.

An apple a day keeps

the doctor away.

Self assessment

How many a's did you write on this page?

Circle your best a.

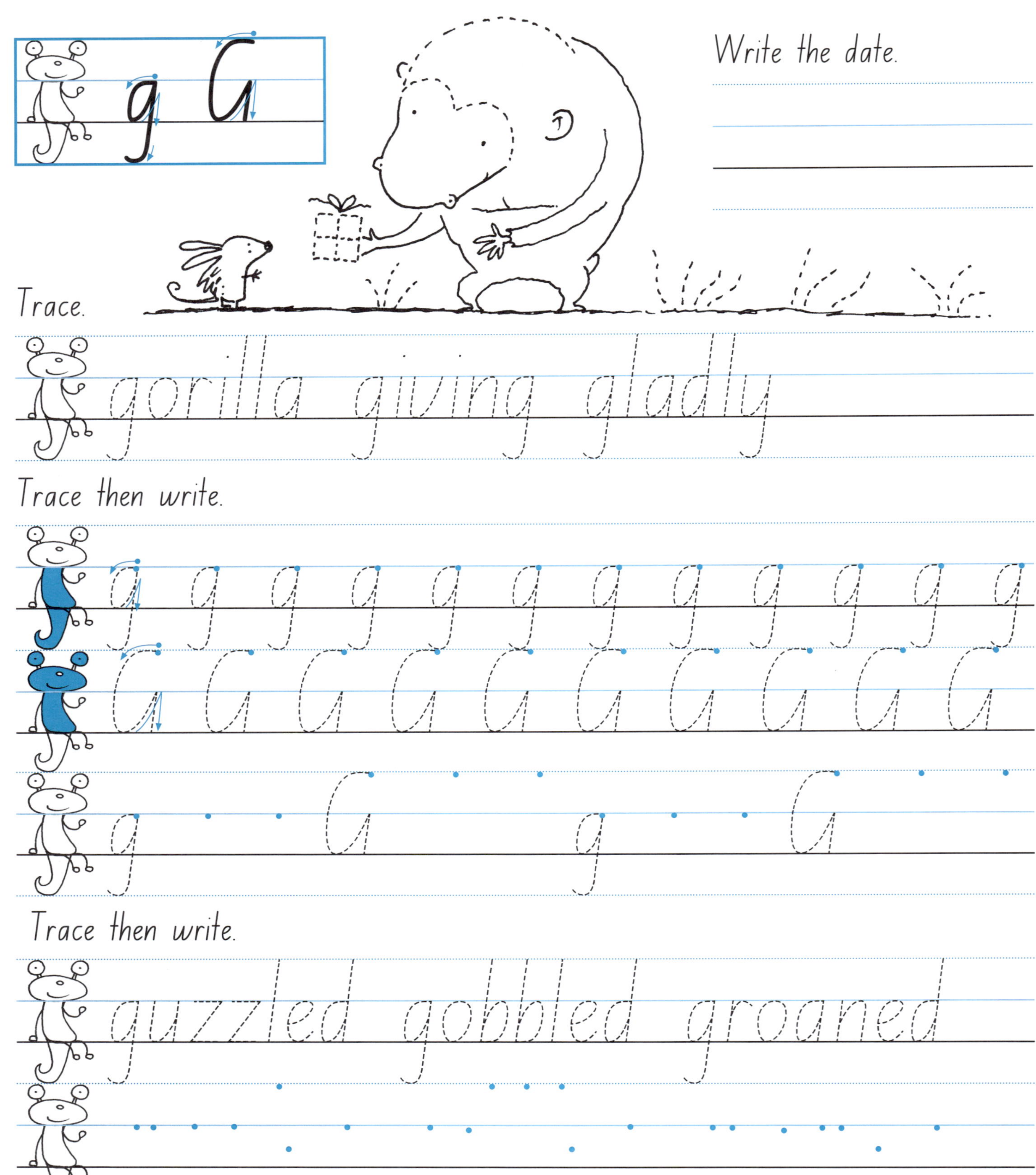

Handwriting: anticlockwise ellipse, long letter (g).
Grammar: nouns, verbs, adverb (gladly), past tense (-ed), question, question word (Why?).
Punctuation: full stop, question mark, upper-case letter to start a sentence.

Spelling and vocabulary: fight, fright, knight, sight, giving, gladly, gobbled, gorilla, groaned, guzzled, silent k (knight), suffixes -ly, -ing, -ed (gladly, giving, groaned).
Literary elements: riddle, joke, word play, homophones (night/knight).

Trace and finish the pattern.

eeleel

Write the date.

Find and trace a in some of these letters.

g b d q d g h b m q g

Trace then write.

Why do dragons sleep

all day? So they can go

fight knights.

Self assessment

Draw a frame around your best g on these two pages.

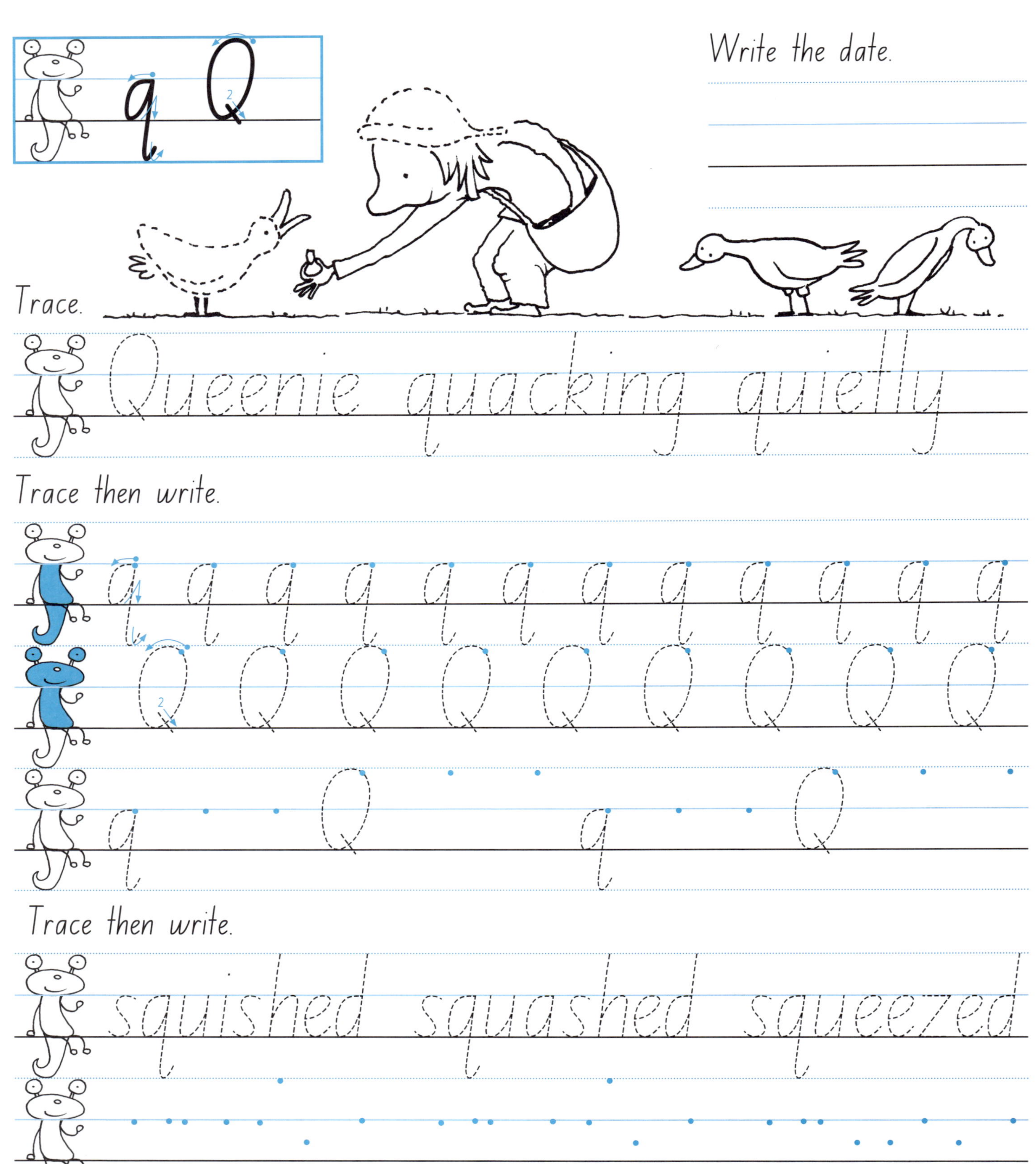

Handwriting: anticlockwise ellipse, long letter (q).
Grammar: proper noun (Queenie), action verbs in the past tense (squished, squashed, squeezed), saying verb (quacking), adverb (quietly), question, question word (What?).
Punctuation: full stop, question mark, upper-case letter to start a sentence.
Spelling and vocabulary: apostrophe for contraction (I've), qu and squ (quacking, quietly, quilt, squashed, squeezed, squished), suffixes -ing, -ily, -ed (quacking, quietly, squished).
Literary elements: riddle, word play (quilt/covered).

Trace and finish the pattern.

Write the date.

elel

Find and trace the long letters.

q v g y w q a g v w a

Trace then write.

What did the quilt say

to the bed? I've got you

covered.

Circle the q with the best tail. Underline the q's you could improve.

Handwriting: anticlockwise ellipse, short letter (c).
Grammar: nouns, action verbs (cutting, crept), saying verbs (croaked, called), adverb (cleverly), irregular verb (creep/crept), question, question word (What?), proper nouns (Mama, Baby, Pop).
Punctuation: question mark, upper-case letter to start a sentence.

Spelling and vocabulary: apostrophe for contraction (where's), called, camel, cleverly, corn, creep, crept, croaked, cutting, popcorn.
Literary elements: riddle, joke, word play, onomatopoeia (croak).

Trace and finish the pattern.

Write the date.

Write the matching upper-case letters.

a u q g w c y

Trace then write.

What did Baby corn say

to Mama corn? Where's

Pop corn?

Draw a frame around your best c and your best C on these two pages.

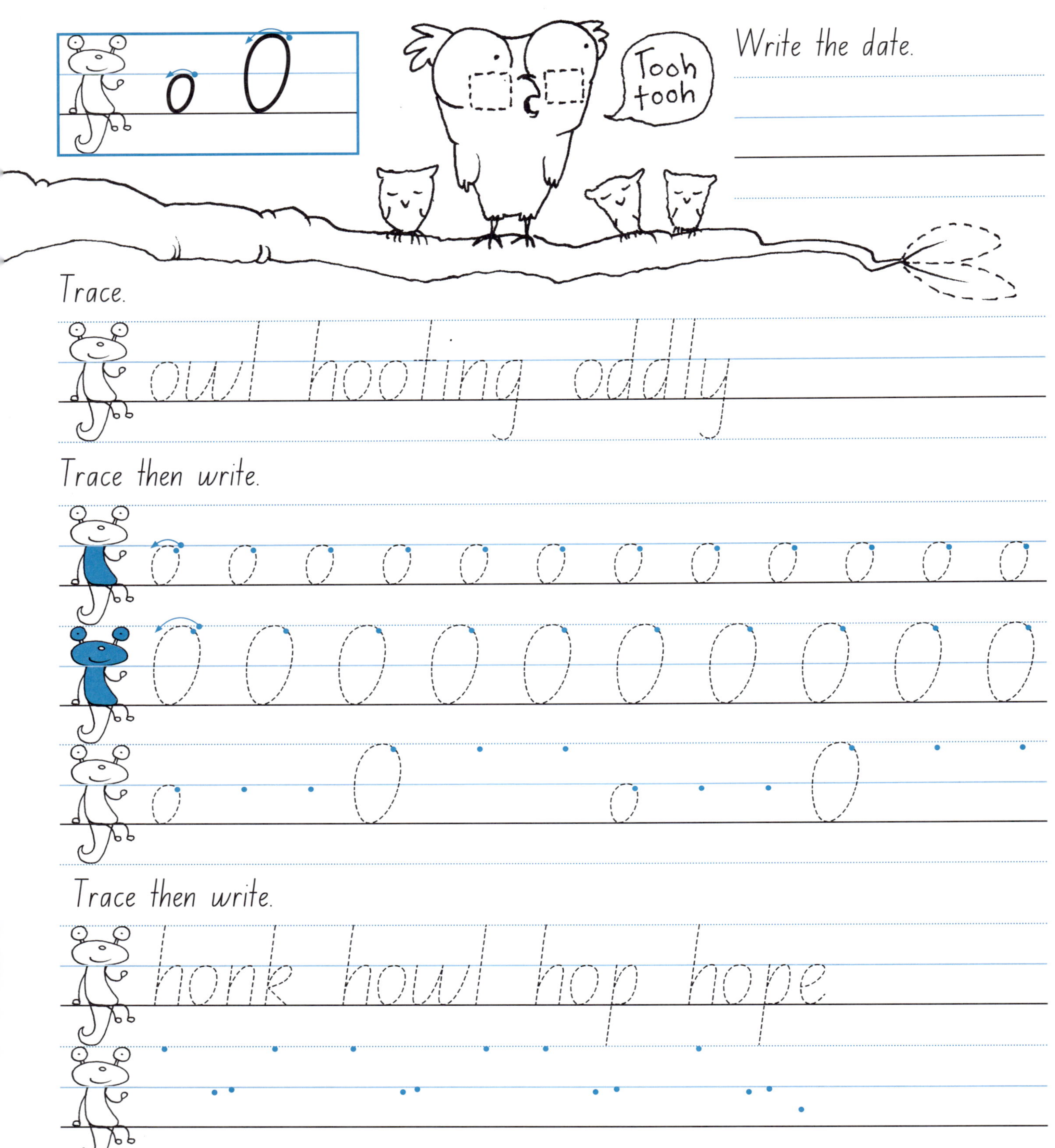

Handwriting: anticlockwise ellipse, short letter (o).
Grammar: nouns, gender nouns (cow/bull), saying verbs (hoot, howl, honk), adverb (oddly), question, question word (What?), irregular verb (does/do).
Punctuation: question mark, upper-case letter to start a sentence.
Spelling and vocabulary: 'ow' (cow, howl, owl), 'oo' (hooting, moo), honk, hop, hope, oddly.
Literary elements: riddle, joke, word play (moo-vies), onomatopoeia (hoot, howl, honk).

Trace and finish the pattern.

Write the date.

Trace then write.

What does the cow like

to do on her day off?

Go to the moo-vies.

Circle the o on each page that has the best shape.

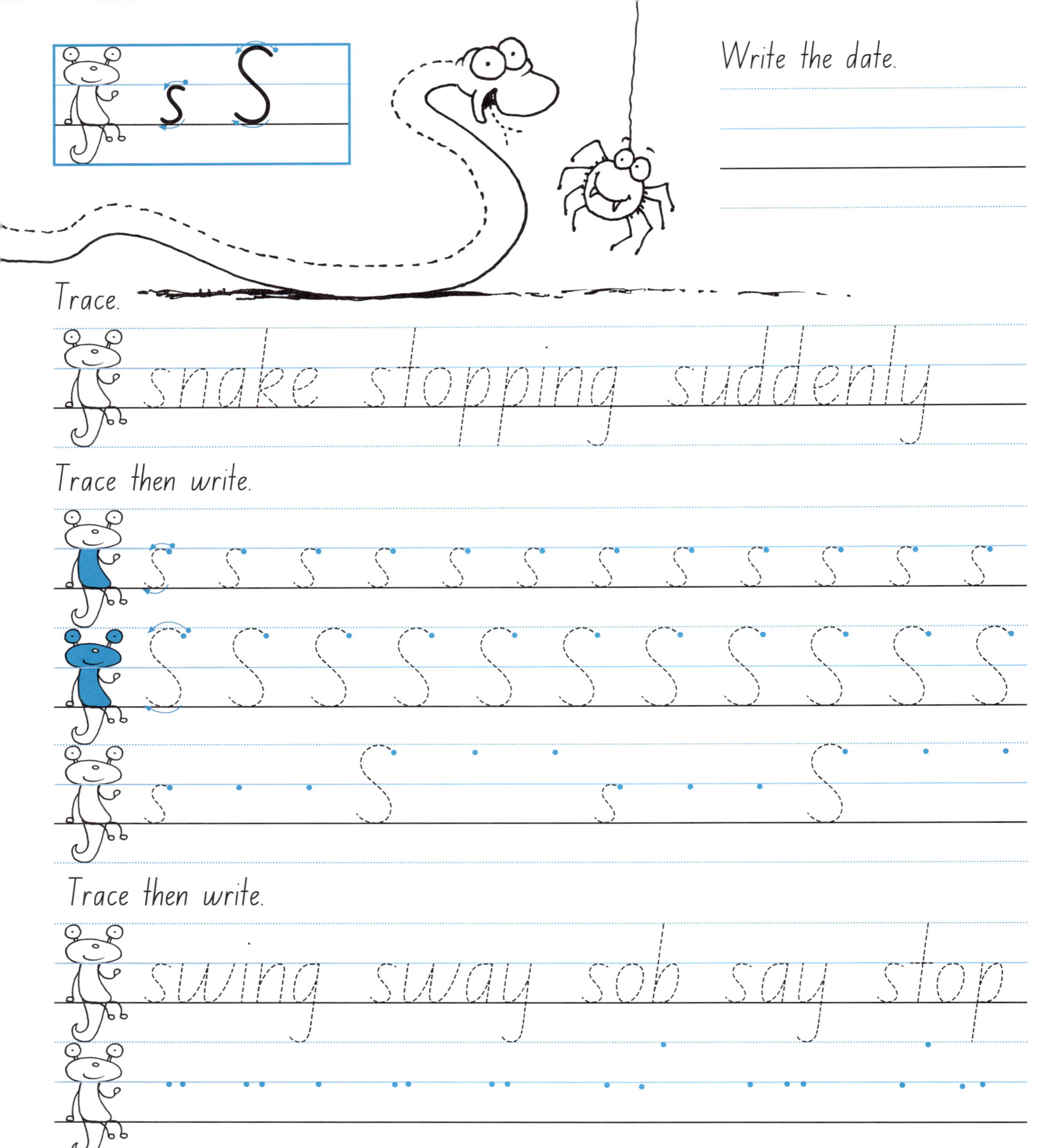

Handwriting: anticlockwise ellipse, short letter (s).
Grammar: noun, action verbs (stopping, swing, sway), saying verbs (sob, say), adverb (suddenly), statement, word families (stop/stopped/stopping).
Punctuation: full stop, upper-case letter to start a sentence.

Spelling and vocabulary: when to double final consonant to add -ing (stopping), blends with s: sn (snake), st (stop, sticks, stones), sw (sway, swing), word families (stop, stopping), suffix -ly, (suddenly).
Literary elements: rhyme (say/sway), children's rhyme (dated to 1862).

Trace and finish the pattern.

Write the date.

Trace then write.

Sticks and stones may

break my bones but words

will never hurt me.

Draw a square around the word that shows your best handwriting.

Handwriting: anticlockwise ellipse, tall letter (d).
Grammar: noun, action verbs (dive, drop, drag, droop), adverb (daintily), question, question word (When?).
Punctuation: question mark, upper-case letter to start a sentence.

Spelling and vocabulary: daintily, dancing, dingo, dinosaur, dive, dragged, droop, drop, sore, when to double final consonant to add suffix -ed (drag, dragged). The word "dingo" is based on the word "dingu" from the Dharug and Dharawal languages. It means "wild dog".
Literary elements: riddle, joke, word play (dinosaur/sore).

Trace and finish the pattern.

eelee

Write the date.

Find and trace d in some of these letters.

d f h d l k m d p a h f d

Trace then write.

When do dinosaurs need

bandages? When they get

dino-sores.

Self assessment

Draw a tick above every d on this page. Circle your best d.

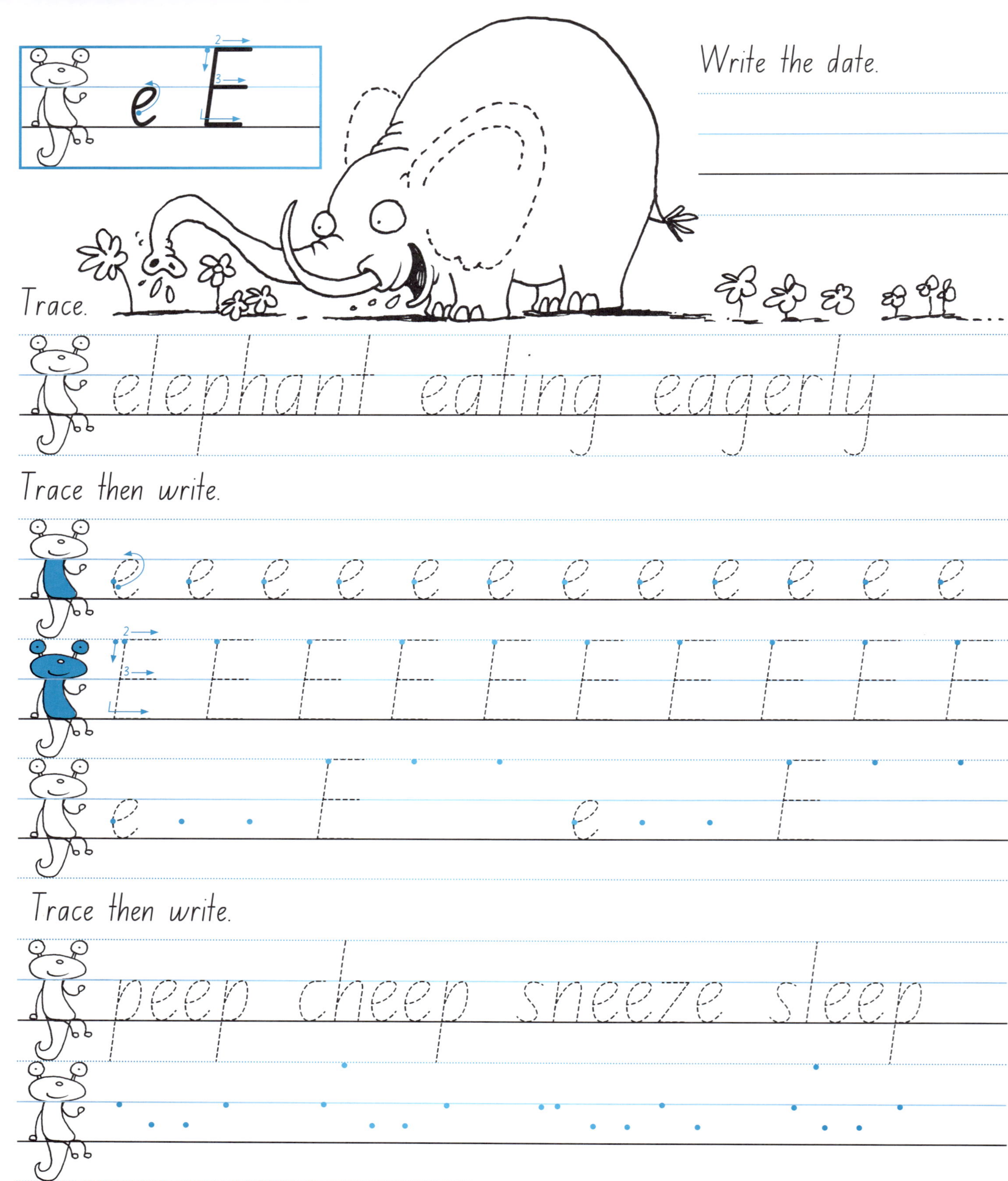

Handwriting: anticlockwise ellipse, short letter (e).
Grammar: nouns, action verbs (sleep, eating), saying verb (cheep), adverb (eagerly), statement.
Punctuation: full stop, upper-case letter to start a sentence.

Spelling and vocabulary: 'ee' (cheep, peep, sleep, sneeze), 'ph' (elephant, phone, photo), rhyme (healthy/wealthy, wise/rise, peep/cheep/sleep).
Literary elements: moral, proverb (published 1735, attributed to Benjamin Franklin), onomatopoeia (cheep).

Trace and finish the pattern.

Write the date.

Trace then write.

Early to bed and early

to rise, makes you healthy,

wealthy and wise.

Draw triangles around three e's with the best shape.

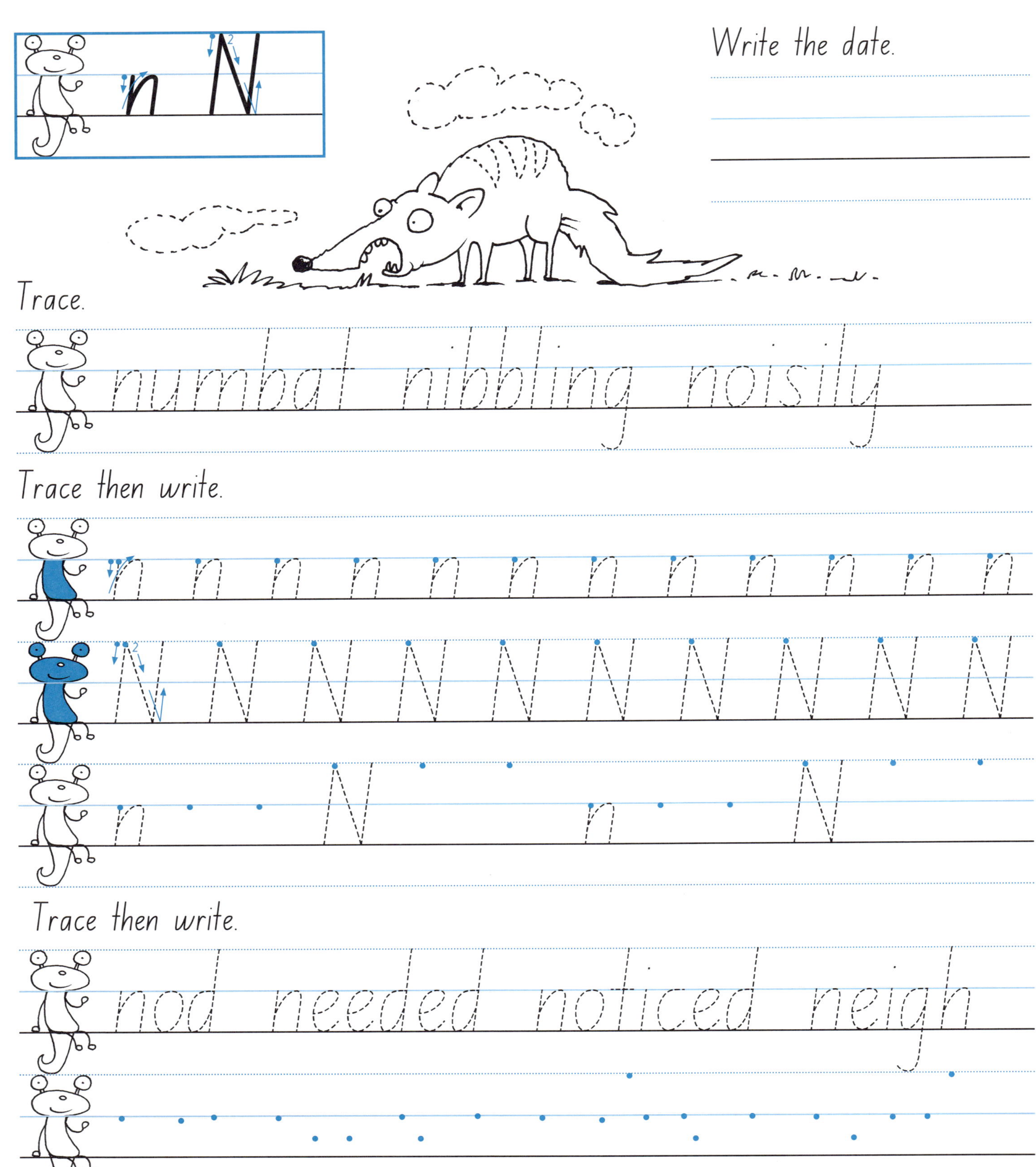

Handwriting: clockwise ellipse, short letter (n).
Grammar: nouns, sensing or thinking verb (needed, noticed), adverb (noisily), statement.
Punctuation: full stop, upper-case letter to start a sentence, possessive apostrophe (sailor's).

Spelling and vocabulary: night, delight, morning, needed, neigh, nibbling, nod, noisily, noticed, numbat, pink, sailor, warning, suffixes -ily, -ing (noisily, warning, nibbling). The word "numbat" is based on the word "noombat" from the Noongar language.
Literary elements: ancient rhyme (over 2000 years old) for weather forecasting, onomatopoeia (neigh), rhyme (night/delight, warning/morning).

Trace and finish the pattern.

Write the date.

Trace then write.

Pink in the morning, a

sailor's warning. Pink in

the night, a sailor's delight.

Self assessment

How many n's did you write on this page?

Draw a square around an n you could improve.

Handwriting: clockwise ellipse, short letter (r).
Grammar: nouns, action verbs (riding, rub, roll, rush, ripped), adverb (rapidly), conjunction (because), question, question word (Why?).
Punctuation: question mark, upper-case letter to start a sentence, upper-case for sounds (aRRR), exclamation mark.

Spelling and vocabulary: pirate, press, rat, rapidly, red, rest, riding, ripped, rock, roll, room, rub, rug, rush.
Literary elements: riddle, joke, word play, onomatopoeia (aRRR), rhyme (are/aRRR).

Trace and finish the pattern.

Write the date.

Write.

r R

Use r to finish these words. Trace the words.

ug oom ed p ess est

Trace then write.

Why are pirates called

pirates? Because they aRRR!

Self assessment

How many R's are on these two pages?

Circle your best capital R.

Handwriting: clockwise ellipse, short letter (m).
Grammar: plural noun (meerkats), proper nouns (Mars, Martian), verbs, adverb (merrily), adjectives (soft, white), question, question word (What's?).
Punctuation: question mark, upper-case letter to start a sentence.

Spelling and vocabulary: apostrophe for contraction (what's), meerkat, mind, missed, move, naming nationalities (Mars/Martian, Earth/Earthling, Australia/Australians, China/Chinese), suffixes -ing, -ly, -ed (munching, merrily, moped)
Literary elements: riddle, joke, word play (marshmallow/Martian-mallow).

Trace and finish the pattern.

Write the date.

Trace then write.

What's soft and white

and lives on Mars?

A Martian-mallow.

Handwriting: clockwise ellipse, tall letter (h).
Grammar: noun, verbs, adverb (happily), question, question word (Why?), word families (hop/hops/hopped/hopping).
Punctuation: question mark, upper-case letter to start a sentence.
Spelling and vocabulary: apostrophe for contraction (aren't), when to double final consonant to add suffix -ing or -ed (hopping, hugged, spotted), had, happily, help, hippo, hit, 'e' to make long vowel sound (hide, hope).
Literary elements: riddle, word play (spotted).

Trace and finish the pattern.

Write the date.

Trace then write.

Why aren't leopards any good at hide-and-seek?

They are always spotted.

Draw a star around your best h and around your best H on these two pages.

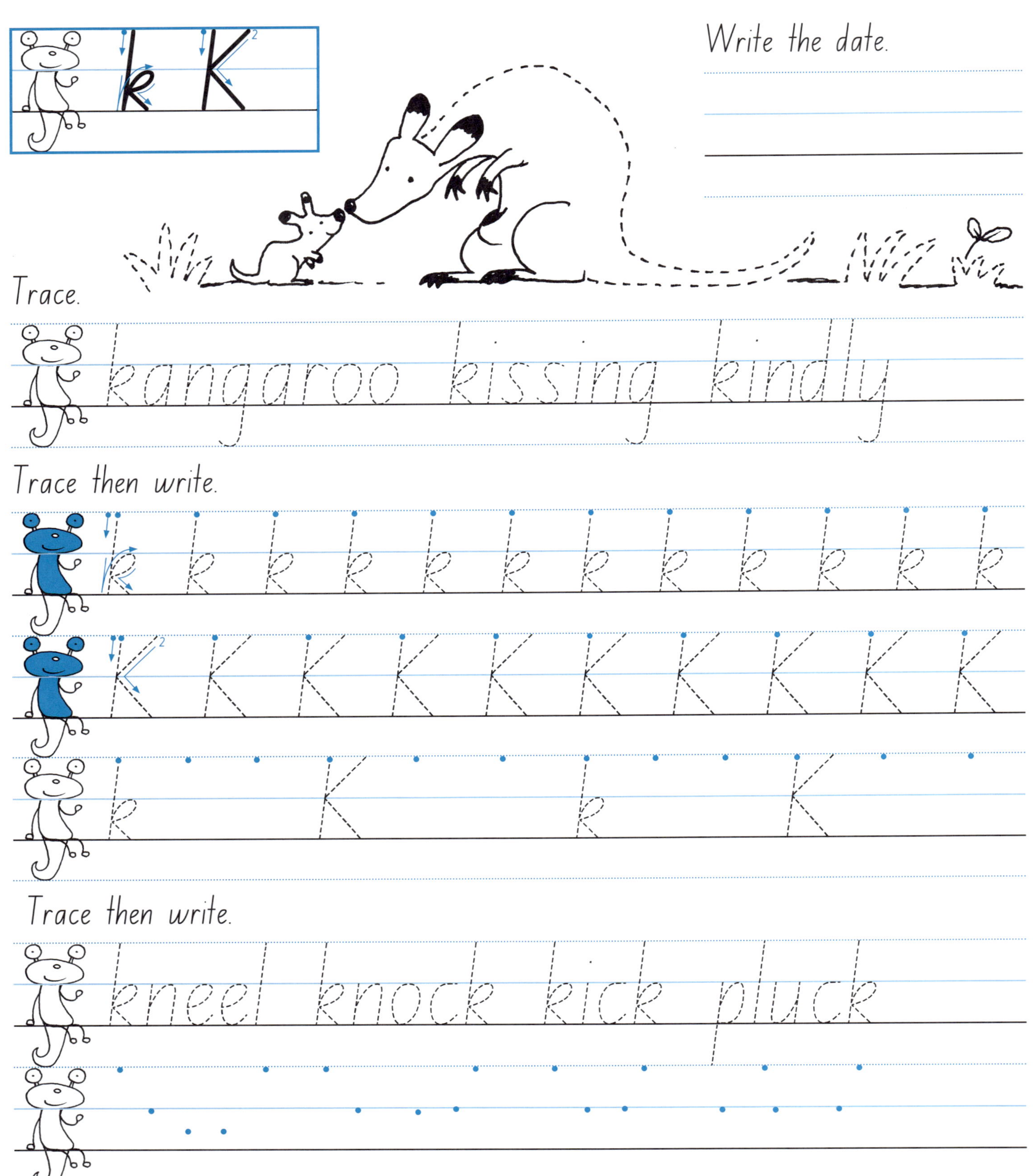

Handwriting: clockwise ellipse, tall letter (k).
Grammar: nouns, action verbs (kneel, kick, kissing), adverb (kindly), statement.
Punctuation: full stop, upper-case letter to start a sentence.

Spelling and vocabulary: 'ck' consonant digraph (kick, knock, pocket, pluck), kangaroo, kindly, kissing, silent 'k' (kneel, knock), change y to i to add -ed (carried). The word "kangaroo" is based on the word "gangurru" from the Guugu Yimithir language.
Literary elements: simile (like a garden), Chinese proverb.

Trace and finish the pattern.

Write the date.

Write.

k K

Trace the letters that start like k.

l b o u y b a x h

Trace then write.

A book is like a garden

carried in the pocket.

Self assessment

How many k's did you write on this page?

Tick your best k.

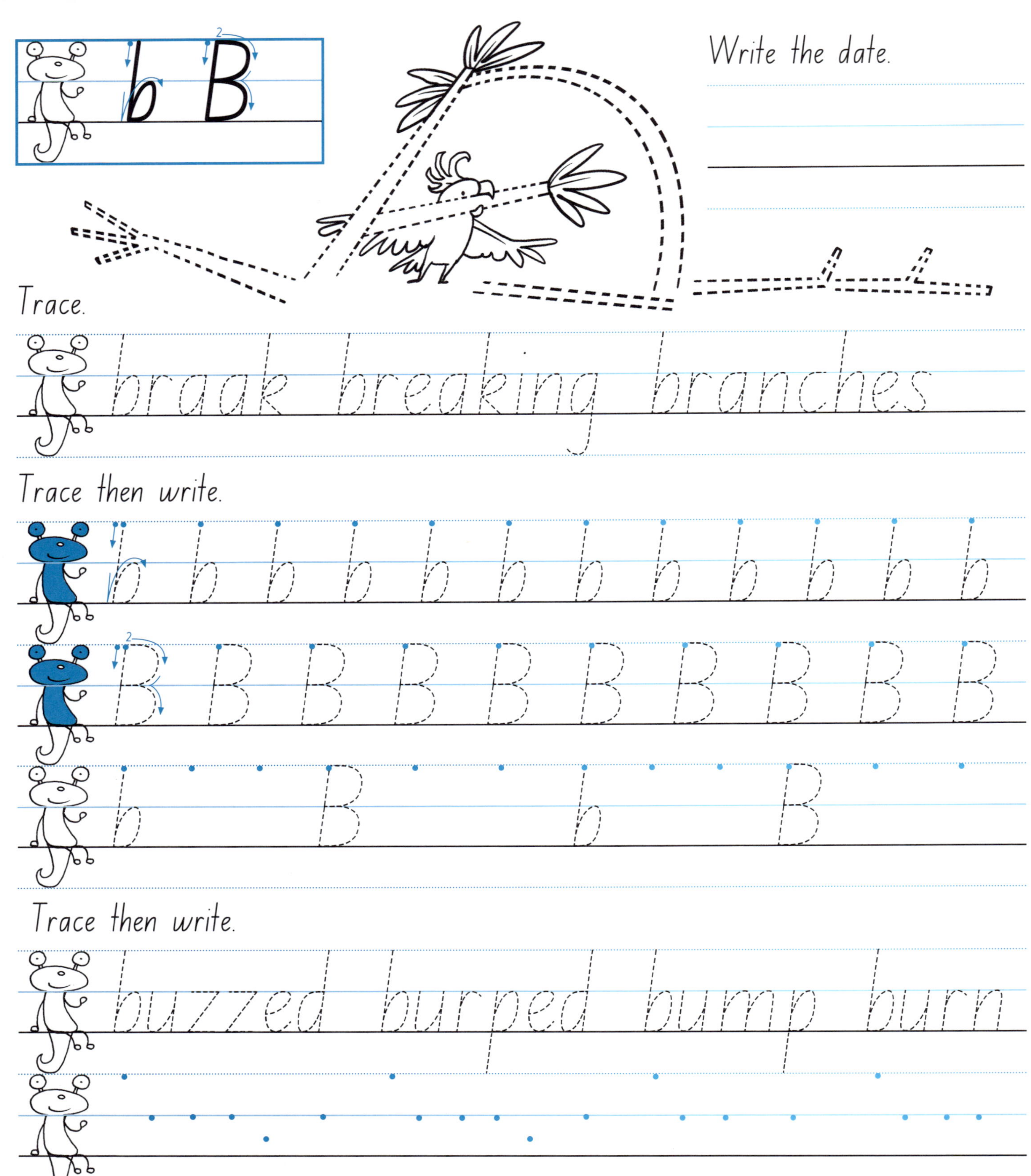

Handwriting: clockwise ellipse, tall letter (b).
Grammar: proper noun (Bob), action verb (breaking), saying verbs (buzzed, burped), question, question word (Why?).
Punctuation: question mark, upper-case letter to start a sentence.

Spelling and vocabulary: battery, braak, because, branches, breaking, bump, bury, buzzed, 'ur' vowel digraph (burped, burn). The word "braak" is from the Gunai-Kurnai language. It means "sulphur-crested cockatoo".
Literary elements: riddle, joke, word play (died), onomatopoeia (buzz, burped).

Trace and finish the pattern.

Write the date.

Find and trace b in these letters.

d p b d b p h b d k b d b d

Trace then write.

Why did Bob bury his

torch? Because the battery

died.

Draw a frame around your best B on these two pages.

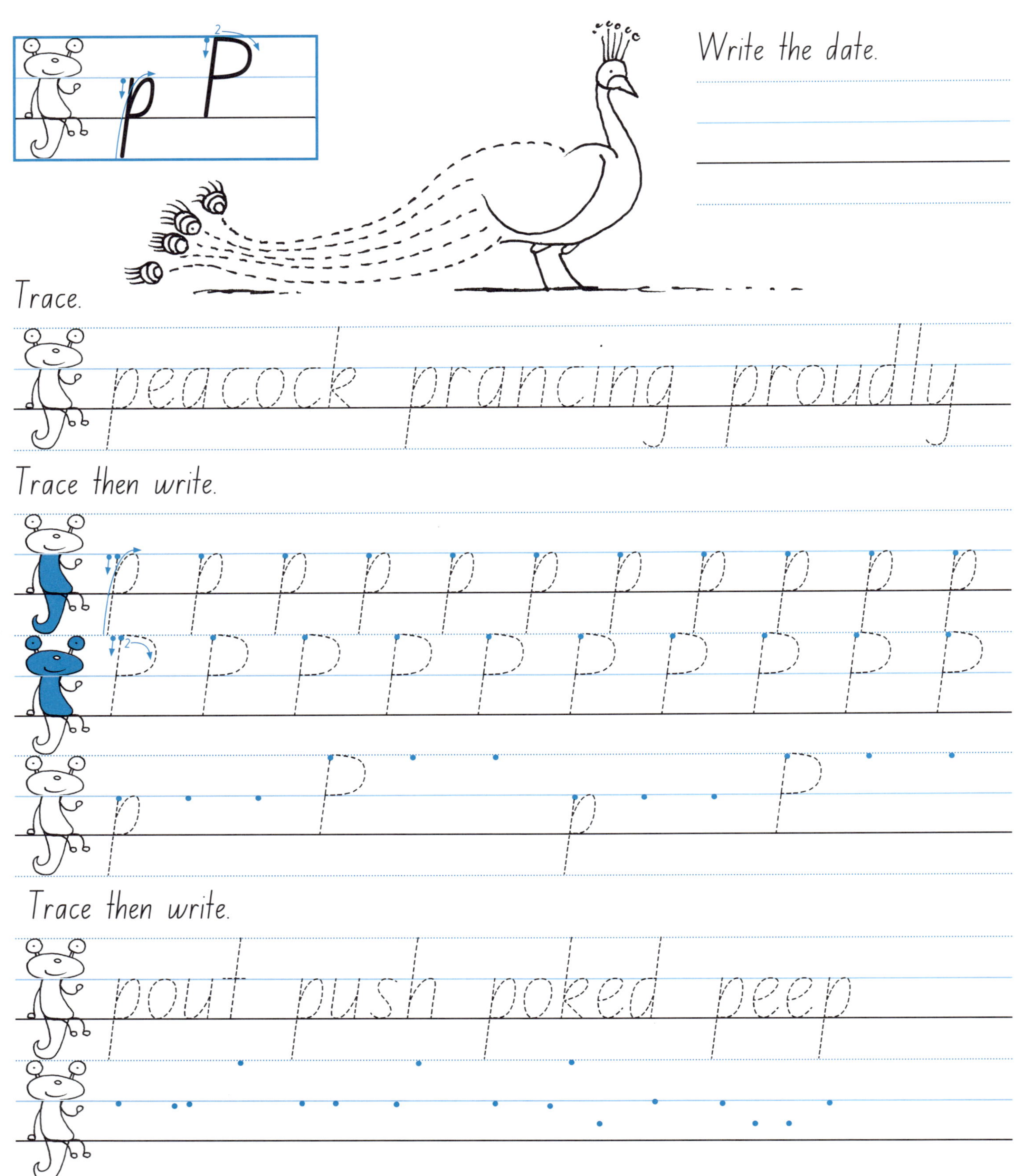

Handwriting: clockwise ellipse, long letter (p).
Grammar: nouns, action verbs (push, poked, prancing), adverb (proudly), statement, command starting with a verb (Be).
Punctuation: full stop, upper-case letter to start a sentence.
Spelling and vocabulary: apostrophe for contraction (you've), male and female words (peacock/peahen), peep, poked, pout, proudly, soft 'c' (prancing, dancing, fancy, ice).
Literary elements: moral (a bird in the hand is worth two in the bush, from various origins including Aesop's fable 'The Hawk and the Nightingale').

Trace and finish the pattern.

Write the date.

Write.

p P

Write the matching upper-case letters.

b k h m r n

Trace then write.

Be happy with what

you've got.

Self assessment

Circle the p with the best tail. Underline the p's you could improve.

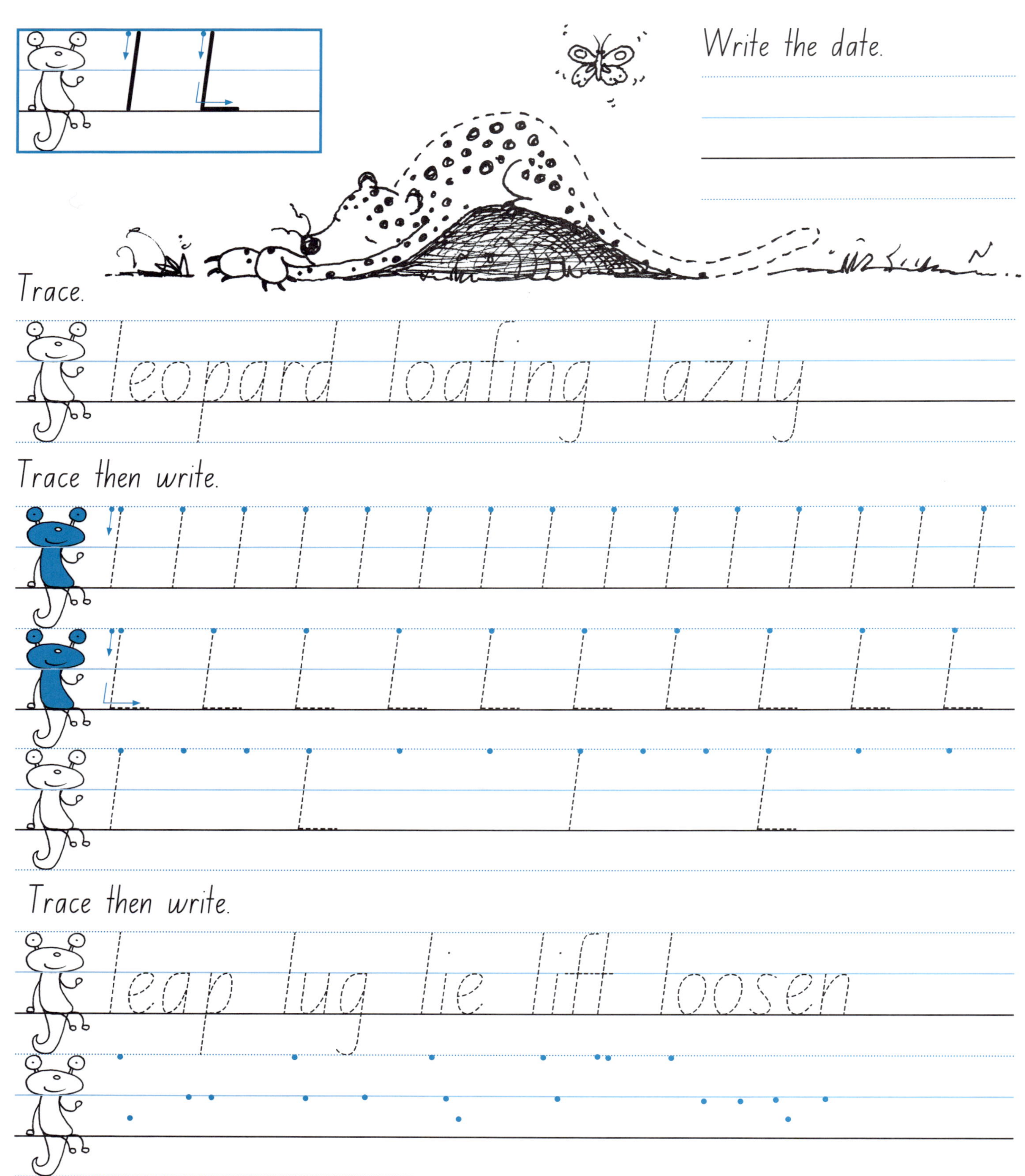

Handwriting: downward diagonal stroke, tall letter (l).
Grammar: nouns, action verbs (leap, lug, lift), adverb (lazily), question, question word (Why?), adjectives (big, wrinkly).
Punctuation: question mark, upper-case letter to start a sentence.

Spelling and vocabulary: apostrophe for contraction (they're), changing y to i to add -ed or -ly (cried, happily, lazily, messily, tried), elephant, leap, leopard, lie, lift, loafing, loosen, lug, wrinkly, homophones (too/to/two).
Literary elements: riddle, joke.

Trace and finish the pattern.

Write the date.

Trace then write.

Why are elephants so

wrinkly? They're too big

to fit on the ironing board.

Are your l's sloping evenly?

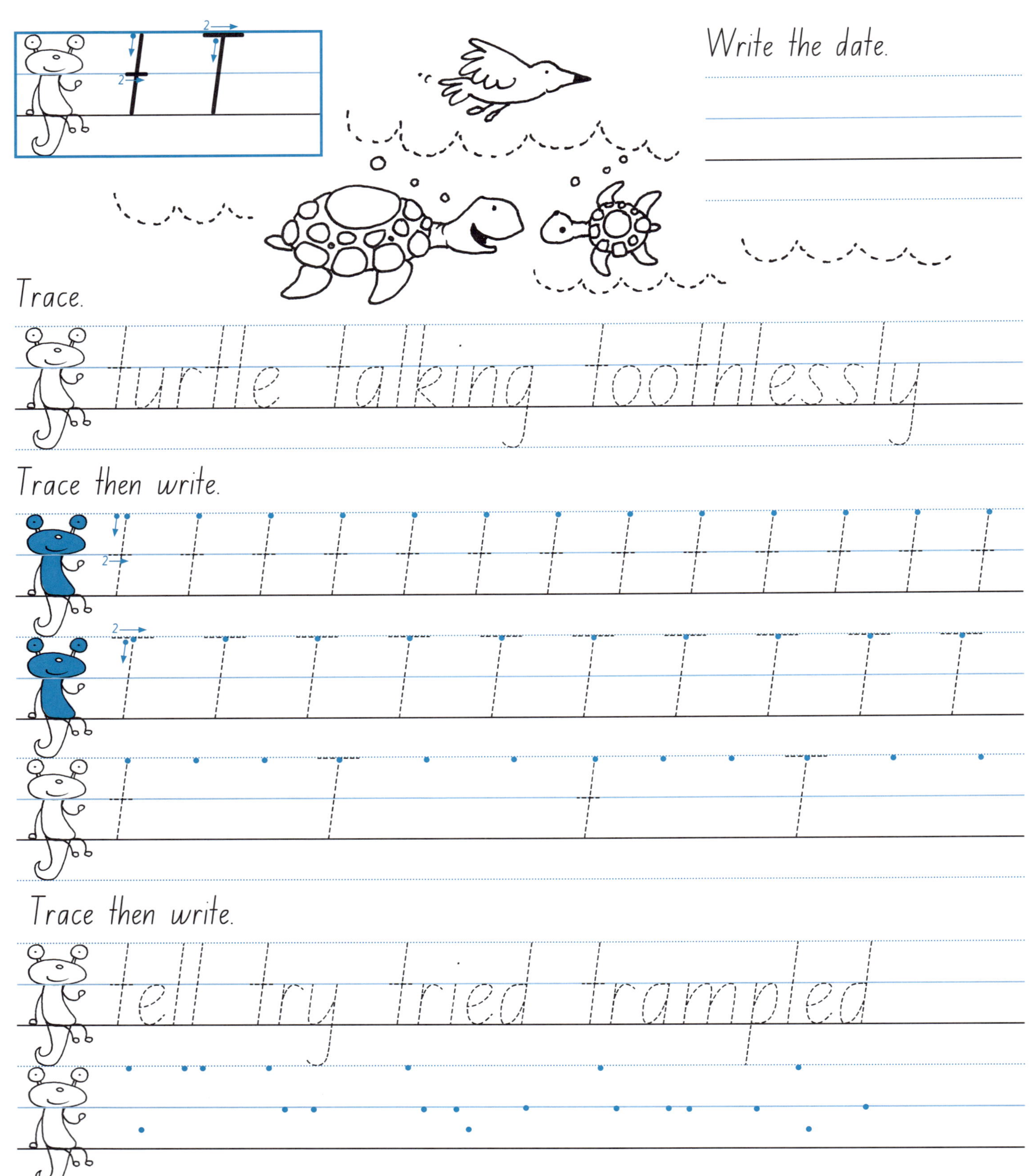

Handwriting: downward diagonal stroke, tall letter (t).
Grammar: nouns, saying verbs (tell, talking), adverb (toothlessly), question, question word (What?).
Punctuation: question mark, upper-case letter to start a sentence.

Spelling and vocabulary: jobs (dentist, doctor, driver, gardener, teacher), suffix -less (toothless, hopeless, helpless), 'th' digraph (thirty, three, throw, tooth), 'wh' digraph (when, what), word families (try/tried).
Literary elements: riddle, joke, word play (tooth hurty/two thirty).

Trace and finish the pattern.

Write the date.

Find and trace the tall letters.

t m l T k p n o q h

Trace then write.

What time is it when

you go to the dentist?

Tooth hurty.

Self assessment

How many t's are on these two pages?

Draw a star around your best t or T.

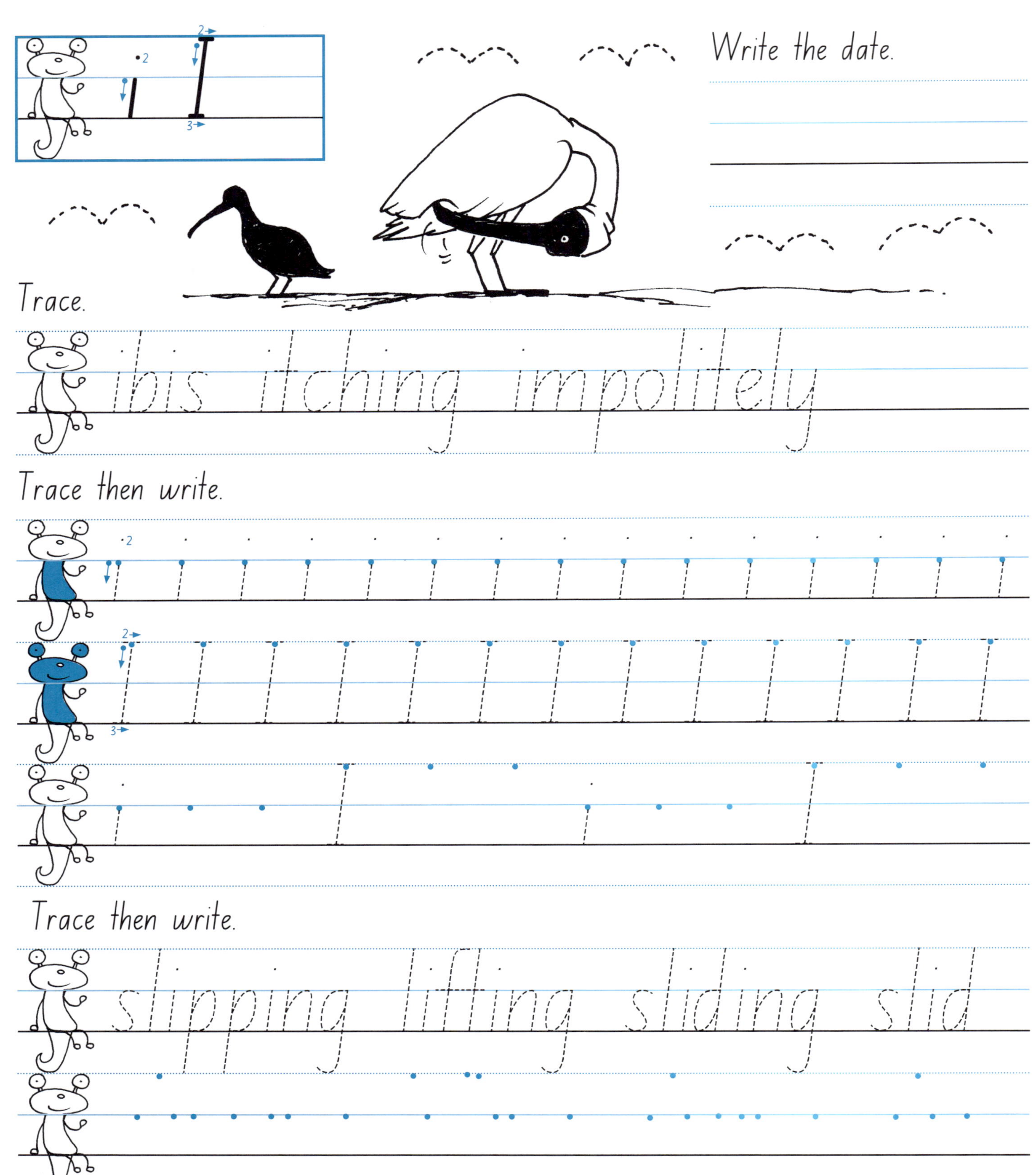

Handwriting: downward diagonal stroke, short letter (i).
Grammar: nouns, action verbs (itching, slipping, lifting, sliding), adverb (impolitely), statement.
Punctuation: full stop, upper-case letter to start a sentence.

Spelling and vocabulary: 'tch' trigraph (ditch, itch, switch, twitch), drop 'e' to add -ing (hiding, riding, sliding), 'nk' blend (drink, link, pink, stink), prefix im- (immature, impolite, impossible), word families (slid/slide/sliding), rhyme (drink/link/pink/stink, later/alligator, while/crocodile).
Literary elements: colloquialism/sayings and expressions.

Trace and finish the pattern.

Write the date.

Write.

i I

Use i to finish these words. Trace the words.

nk drnk pnk stnk lnk

Trace then write.

See you later alligator.

In a while crocodile.

Are your letters sloping evenly?

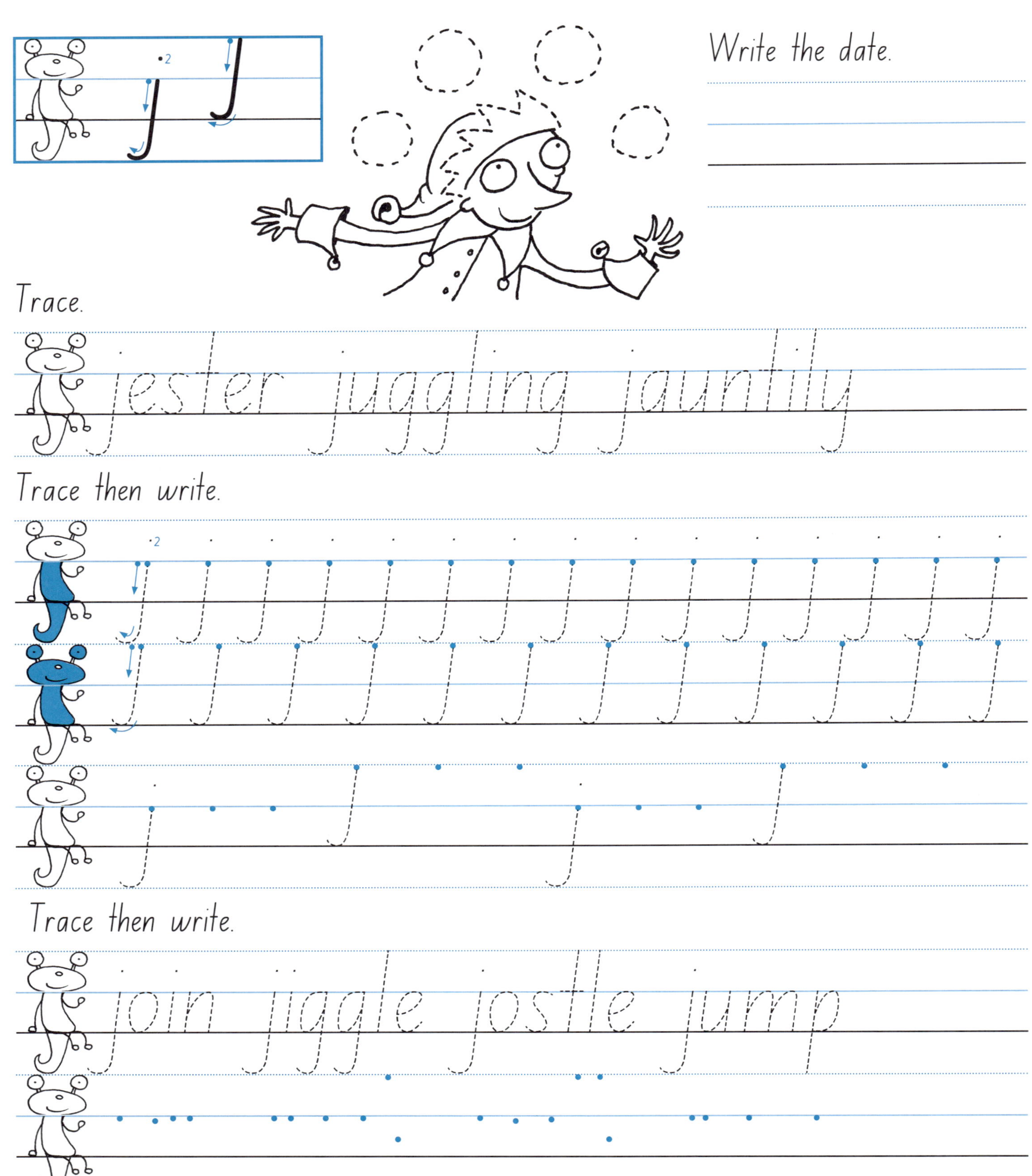

Handwriting: downward diagonal stroke, long letter (j).
Grammar: nouns, action verbs (jiggle, jostle, jump, juggle), adverb (jauntily), statement.
Punctuation: full stop, upper-case letter to start a sentence.

Spelling and vocabulary: jauntily, jester, join, journey, jump, 'le' ending (jiggle, jostle, juggle, single), 'th' digraph (thousand, with).
Literary elements: Chinese proverb.

Trace and finish the pattern.

Write the date.

Find and trace the long letters.

j h m p n q g s c j l

Trace then write.

The journey of a thousand

miles starts with a single

step.

Self assessment

How many j's did you write on these two pages?

Circle your best j and J.

Handwriting: downward diagonal stroke, tall letter (f).
Grammar: nouns, action verbs (fly, fling, floating), adverb (freely), question, question word (What?), proper nouns (Friday, Frank).
Punctuation: question mark, upper-case letter to start a sentence.

Spelling and vocabulary: 'ch' digraph (chases), when to double final consonant to add -ed (flopped, flapped, stopped, hopped), 'fl' blend (fling, floating, flopped), 'sh' digraph (fish).
Literary elements: riddle, joke, word play.

Trace and finish the pattern.

Write the date.

Write.

f F

Use f or F to finish these words. Trace the words.

riday inger rank irst

Trace then write.

What kind of fish chases

a mouse? A catfish.

Highlight or underline ALL the f's on this page.
Circle your best f.

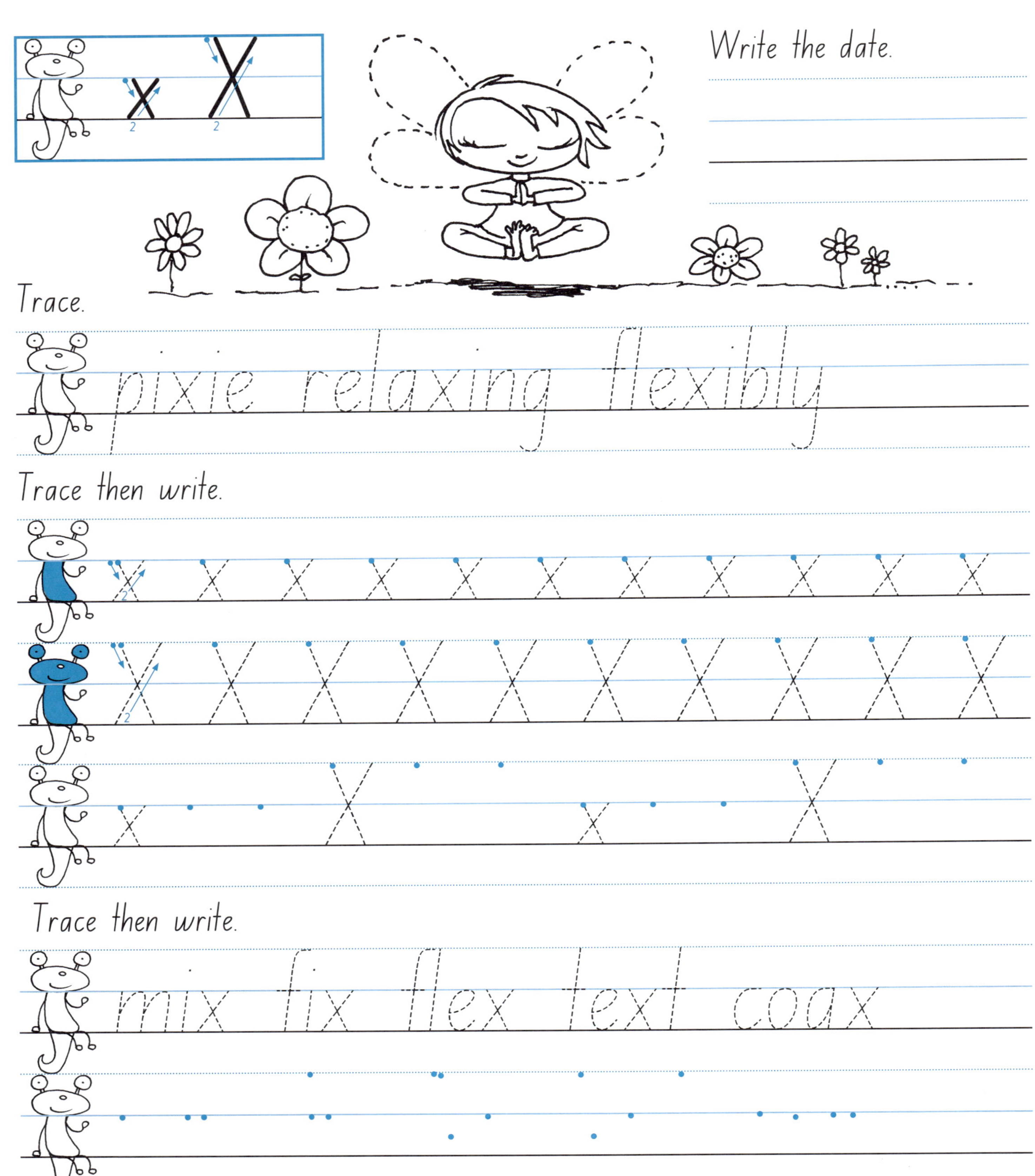

Handwriting: downward diagonal stroke, short letter (x).
Grammar: nouns, action verbs (fix, flex, mix, relaxing), adverb (flexibly), statement, word families (flex/flexible/flexibly/flexed/flexing/inflexible).
Punctuation: full stop, upper-case letter to start a sentence.
Spelling and vocabulary: fix, flex, flexibly, mix, 'oa' vowel digraph (coax, float, boat, groan, moan), pixie, relaxing, stubborn, text.
Literary elements: Aesop fable 'The Reed and the Olive Tree', moral: It is better to be flexible than stubborn.

Trace and finish the pattern.

Write the date.

Write.

x X

Use x to finish these words. Trace the words.

bo fo gala y inde o

Trace then write.

It is better to be

flexible than stubborn.

Tick your five best x's. Draw a square around an x you could improve.

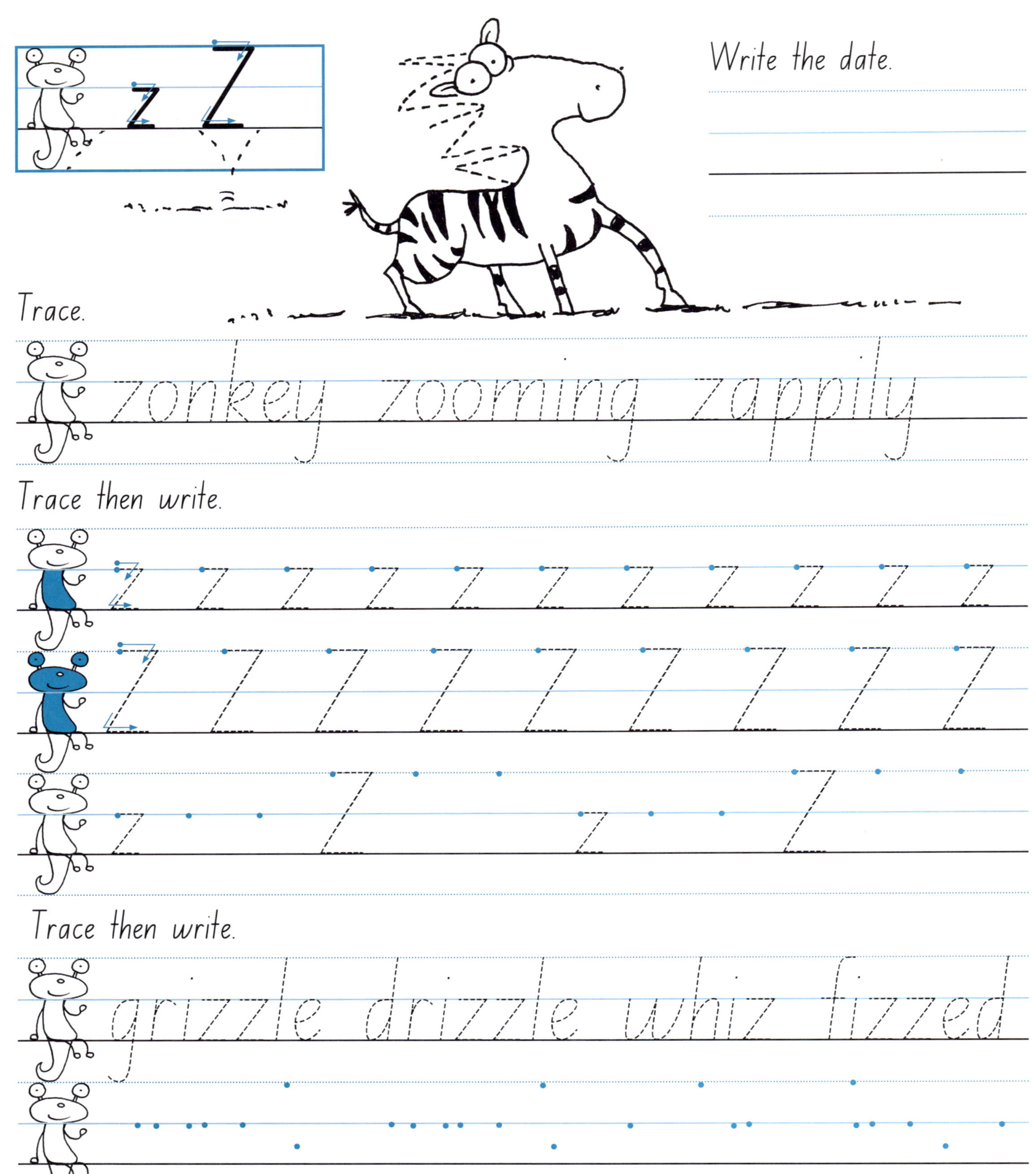

Handwriting: downward diagonal stroke, short letter (z).
Grammar: nouns, verbs, adverb (zappily), question, question word (How?).
Punctuation: question mark, upper-case letter to start a sentence.
Spelling and vocabulary: drizzle, fizzed, grizzle, 'oo' vowel digraph (school, zooming), whiz, zappily, zonkey, rhyme (grizzle/drizzle).
Literary elements: portmanteau word (zonkey = zebra+donkey), riddle, joke, word play (buzz = bus), onomatopoeia (grizzle, fizzed).

Trace and finish the pattern.

Write the date.

Write.

Write the matching upper-case letters.

f j z x i l t

Trace then write.

How does a bee get to school? In a buzz.

Draw a square around the word that is your best handwriting on each page.

Trace then write.

Write the date.

0 1 2

3 4 5 6 7

8 9 10 11 12

13 14 15 16

17 18 19 20

There are 7 days in a week

and 12 months in a year.

Draw a star around your best numeral.

Draw a triangle around a numeral you could improve.

Trace.

Write the date.

There are 365
days in a year and 366
days in a leap year.
30 days has September,
April, June and November.
All the rest have 31
except February, which has
28 days clear and 29 in
each leap year.

Self assessment

Draw a frame around each numeral.
Tick the numeral with the highest value.
How many words name months of the year?

Write the date.

Trace then write.

10 ten 20 twenty 30 thirty

40 forty 50 fifty 60 sixty

70 seventy 80 eighty

90 ninety 100 one hundred

Circle and label your BEST handwriting on this page as 1st, 2nd or 3rd.

Trace then write in correct NUMBER order.

fifty sixty forty

Write the date.

Trace then link the numeral to the number word.

thirty 8 eighty 9 90 seventy

70 nine 80 eight 30 ninety

Trace then write in correct ALPHABETICAL order.

twelve fifteen eleven

Trace then write in correct ALPHABETICAL order.

twenty eighteen nineteen

Draw a box around the neatest handwritten word.

Draw a circle around the best handwritten numeral.

top body line

main line

Write the date.

When you start to join letters, an **exit kick** will help you get from one letter to the next without lifting your pencil.

Track.

a a a a d d d d

h h h h i i i i

k k k k l l l l

m m m m n n n n

t t t t u u u u

Trace.

a d h i k l m n t u

Underline the letter you think will be easiest to write with an exit kick. Circle the letter you think will be hardest to write with an exit kick.

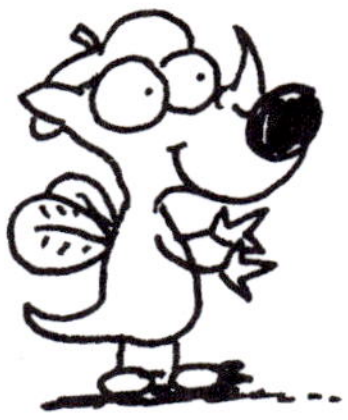

An **exit kick** is a quick, smooth change in direction on a letter that finishes on the main line.

Write the date.

Trace then write.

a a d d

h h i i

k k l l

m m n n

t t u u

How many words can you make using only the letters above? Write the words on the lines. Don't forget the exit kicks.

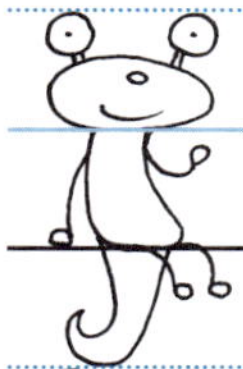

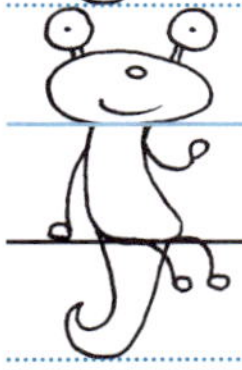

Self assessment

Are your exit kicks smooth?

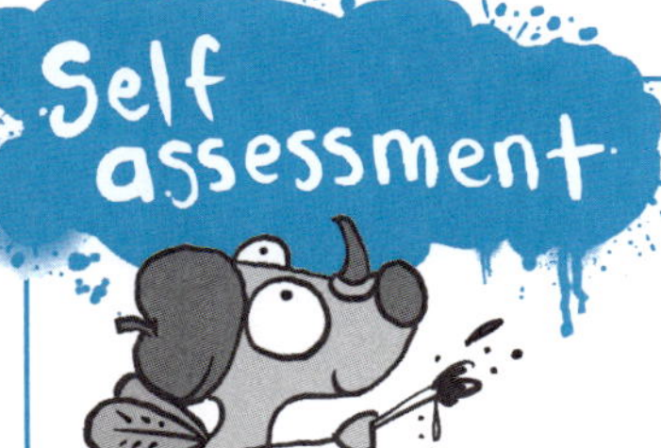

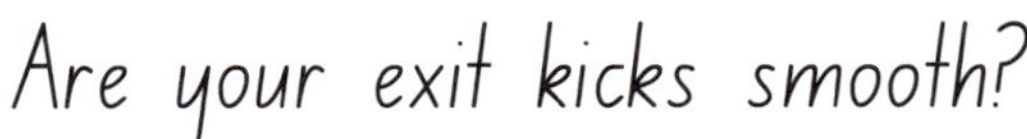

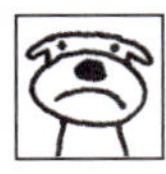

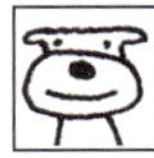

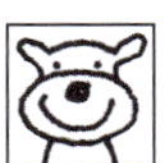

top body line
main line

Write the date.

The letters v and w finish at the top body line. Instead of an exit kick, they have an **exit hook**.

Track.

v v v v v v v v v

w w w w w w w w

v v v v v v v v v

w w w w w w w w

Trace.

v w v w v w v w v w

Trace then write.

v v v

w w w

Circle your best exit hook.

When you start to join letters, an **entry** will help you get from one letter to the next with some letters.

Write the date.

Track.

i i i i j j j j

m m m m n n n n

p p p p r r r r

u u u u v v v v

w w w w y y y y

Trace.

i j m n p r u v w y

Self assessment

Circle the letters that have both an entry **and** an exit.

Remember! Upper-case letters don't join to other letters so they **don't** have entries or exits. You also don't need an entry at the start of a word.

Write the date.

Trace then write.

i i

j j

m m

n n

p p

r r

u u

v v

w w

y y

Trace.

Boing

If you can't beat them, join them.

Self assessment

Are your entries smooth?

Progressive assessments

Each term, write the sentence.
Colour the stars to rate your handwriting.
See how your handwriting improves!

The quick brown fox jumps over the lazy dog.

Term 1 Date ______________

Rating ☆ ☆ ☆ ☆ ☆

Term 2 Date ______________

Rating ☆ ☆ ☆ ☆ ☆

Progressive assessments continued

The quick brown fox jumps over the lazy dog.

Term 3 Date ______

Rating ☆ ☆ ☆ ☆ ☆

Term 4 Date ______

Rating ☆ ☆ ☆ ☆ ☆